MACRAMÉ

MACRAMÉ

BY BETTY ALFERS

GEORGE G. HARRAP & CO. LTD
London   Toronto   Wellington   Sydney

Printed in Great Britain by
Redwood Press Limited
Trowbridge, Wiltshire

Contents

Introduction

Examine a single knot and you will find that it has dimension, texture and some very interesting designs. Soon you may find yourself thinking of knots as ornamental, rather than merely functional. That is what happened very long ago and far away . . . and that is how macramé was born.

Originally, the term referred only to the fringe on an Arabic scarf or shawl, but today it represents the entire field of decorative knotting . . . an art that can be learned almost overnight by anyone from 9 to 90. And, once the basic knots are mastered, the creative designs and uses for macramé are almost endless. So here is macramé, a highly satisfying, enjoyable way to spend random hours, and gain spectacular results and envious compliments.

Betty Alfers

MACRAMÉ

Macramé ?

Macramé is the art of decorative knotting — using a series of various knots to produce ornamental trims, fringes and fabrics. It is a very old craft begun at least six centuries ago. Over the years, however, the art fell into wide disuse except for sailors who passed long, dull hours at sea knotting heavy twine into articles which they might sell or trade in foreign ports. Today, macramé accessories are very popular, and since almost any material may be used — from fine thread which makes what is referred to as macramé lace to leather strips — many do-it-yourselfers are tempted to try their hand at knotting. It is for these anxious artisans that this book has been written.

1

What Will I Need?

Macramé enthusiasts have begun with no more necessary equipment than some string and a handy doorknob — but, in less desperate straits, I would suggest that you obtain at least the following basic working materials:

knotting board — This is merely a firm working base which may be balsa wood, polystyrene board, a sand "pillow", or cork- or card-board covered with strong wrapping paper (the heavy brown paper of large shopping bags works well here). The knotting board should be shaped for easy handling, depending on the size of the project, as well as lightweight and fairly rigid. A very thin slab of foam rubber, for instance, might be made rigid by gluing or otherwise fastening it to a piece of hardboard. A good knotting board, however, must be pliable enough to allow for the easy insertion of holding pins yet it must hold them fast . . . any notice-board material that holds drawing pins should also be perfect as a knotting board. If you plan to make large as well as small macramé items, you might find it convenient to prepare, at the outset, various sizes of knotting board. The handiest seem to be between 12 by 20 inches and 36 by 48 inches, although larger works may call for a larger knotting board. A grid, penciled lightly onto the knotting board, may be of some help in aligning series of knots vertically and/or horizontally.

pins—These are needed to hold the work in position, and must be of stout variety. The ones illustrated throughout are called T-pins, and can be obtained from the supplier mentioned on page 84. Glass-headed or milliner's pins are also suitable. How many you will need will depend on the size of your work, but they are inexpensive, and one half-pound package will usually be enough.

scissors — sharp.

As you progress and go on to bigger and more complicated projects, you may also need rubber bands, a tape measure, yardstick, glue, crochet hooks, sewing or tapestry needles, milliner's pins, beads, wooden embroidery rings and other items — but these are also inexpensive, and the small outlay will be far outweighed by the enjoyment and satisfaction of making your own original necklaces, hangings or belts, or creating a gift to give to a friend.

The Materials

Although they can be used (as in our Beaded Yarn Necklace project), knitting yarns are not the best material for macramé knotting — the heavier rug yarns, however, being less stretchy and springy, are fine. For such outdoor items as hangings and cords, the stiff twine that you find in hardware stores is very good. And sisal is perfect for any open, net-like items such as shopping bags, hanging plant holders and skirt trims. The new plastic twine, which now comes in a wide range of colors, is also very effective, and is readily available in most local hardware or supply stores. The thickness of jute twine gives quick results and is a very inexpensive material. You might alternatively use soutache, cotton or rayon cord, leather thongs, ribbon, common household string, and many other kinds of knotting material. These are only a few suggestions, but a little thought and imagination will certainly uncover many other possibilities. For instance, even the thin, multicolored strands of telephone wire may be used. Keep your eye open for macramé materials available around your house. You may be pleasantly surprised.

Using Color

Natural, earth colors, like brown, beige and tan, are enormously popular today, but the bright colors — pink and orange, purple and lime — have not been forgotten. Although macramé cord is not yet available in a wide range of color, as are knitting and needlework yarns, handicraft suppliers are beginning to stock cord and twine of various kinds and colors for use in macramé.

If, however, you are unable to locate the colors you want for a particular project, there's no need to abandon it, or settle for what is available. Sisal, cotton and nylon twine, for instance, take relatively well to dye. You can buy a ball of off-white sisal twine, cut from it the various lengths you need, and dye them any color you want. Be sure, however, to follow the manufacturer's directions for using the various dyes available.

Heavy manila is a bit too thick to take dye well, but the natural manila coloring looks especially well and interesting decorated or bound by heavy, brightly colored knitting or rug yarn.

While you are practicing the many knots in this book, try to visualize how they would look using various colors and types of cord. Let your creative juices flow. Soon you will find yourself designing and making colorful, truly original belts and necklaces in minutes.

Getting Ready to Start

The first thing you must do is to find an anchor for your work. This may be a piece of strong line or cord (often called an anchor or holding cord), a dowel-rod, pencil, knitting needle, or some other long, thin, fairly rigid span which may be fixed horizontally at the top of the knotting board. A line of partially inserted nails, push pins or T-pins can also serve to anchor your work, but a holding line is considered best.

Many simple projects can be worked even without a knotting board. All you really need is an anchor and for this even a doorknob will serve. Simply make a knot to hold all the cords together (see page 18 for how to make an Overhand Knot) and fasten the work to a handy doorknob with another piece of cord. Or, slip the knot inside a drawer and close it . . . and you are ready to begin.

How Much Yarn?

As in knitting, crocheting and other such handi-crafts, macramé knotting takes up much more yarn or cord than the length of the piece you plan to make. Although much depends on the thickness of the cord or yarn, and the kinds of knots you use, it is wise to assume that you will need a length of cord at least *eight* times the final length of your proposed piece. Say, for instance, that you want to macramé a string light pull one foot long. You will need eight feet of cord or string. You will then halve the string to find the center, and anchor the center to the holding line — leaving *two* working strands *four* times the length of the completed piece.

As you gain experience, you will be better able to ascertain just how much of the knotting material you will need for the project you have in mind. But, for now, it is better to be safe than sorry — to have material left over than to run short. You can always use it later in another project. It *is* possible to splice cord in macramé. Yarns and the lighter twines do lend themselves quite easily to this. Just place the new length of cord alongside the short one and knot it in just as if there were no break. But the thickness and stiffness of some cord and the type of knots you are including in your project may not lend themselves easily to splicing, so always be careful to get enough and do not cut the cords prematurely.

The fact that so much cord is needed (and the longer the proposed piece the longer the working strands) can cause many problems, from struggling with tangled cords to knocking over a lamp while trying to work the end of a 12-foot strand through a knot loop. A good way of easing the problem is through bundling.

Bundling

Bundling is simply that. It is folding each strand separately so that the end of the strand is within easy reach (12 to 18 inches) of the work being done. Depending on the thickness of the cord or yarn, a bundle can be made by winding the material around two or four fingers, or around an available book — this one perhaps — then slipping the material off and securing it. The idea is to end up with a bundle of cord or yarn that is thin enough to fit through knot loops easily, will not become entangled, and is comfortable to work with. Each bundle may be secured by a rubber band (the small brightly colored ones are perfect since they can be contrasted with the color of your working material and they can hold the cord tightly) or with wire twist ties — the kind used to secure plastic bags, etc. Twist ties work better than rubber bands on the soft types of cord such as knitting wool or rug yarn. Heavy duty rubber bands are a must for the heavy sisal twines.

Working with Beads

For short pieces, adding beads is a simple process — you string a bead onto the appropriate strand as you need it. You may, however, want to use beads on a long belt but find that the length of the cord makes it necessary for you to bundle the strands. To make the bundle work for you, simply string a good number of beads onto each strand you want to sport beads (once you decide on a pattern, you'll have some idea where you'd like to see beads) *before* bundling. Then the bundle itself will hold the beads close to the work and within easy reach. And, as you release more cord, slide the beads on down the line. If you run out of beads before you are finished, simply unbundle, string more beads and rebundle. When you get near the end and bundling is unnecessary, you can revert to the old way of stringing on a single bead as you need it.

To add beads to the ends of strands, dip the strand ends in white or colorless glue and work the ends into the beads (a hatpin or needle may be of help here) then let dry. If the diameter of the bead is too large, an Overhand Knot tied into the cord before glueing should make it snug.

Anchoring

To anchor a cord, after finding the center, work either of the two starting knots — the Lark's Head or the Double Clove Hitch with Picot. In the same way, anchor as many cords as you need to give the piece the desired width. For instance, and depending on the strength and thickness of the material you are using, you might anchor twice for a Yorkshire terrier collar (giving you four working strands), four times for a Bulldog collar, and six times for a Great Dane collar . . . or, once or twice for a pinky ring, and five or six times for a wide belt. Instructions for making the two anchor knots will be found at the beginning of the next section. Believe it or not, you are ready to start!

The Knots

Following is a listing and directions for making 35 different knots, and suggestions for using them in your work. However, before starting on a project, I would suggest that you make up a sampler . . . simply work each knot about three or four times, preferably in different materials — cord, ribbon, yarn, etc. In this way, as well as helping you to learn the various knots, you will get some idea of how the different materials should be handled to get the desired results. When done, the sampler will also serve as a three-dimensional "reference book" to be consulted when you want to see exactly how a certain knot looks when finished.

BASIC SINGLE KNOTS

BASIC CHAINS AND BRAIDS

ORNAMENTAL KNOTS

Anchor Knots

1. Lark's Head — This knot is usually worked in a series anchoring the work to the cord, dowel, etc. which serves as the holding line. The Lark's Head is often used to start work, especially when keeping an exact width is not too important. Place the center of the cord under the holding line, raise the ends up and over the holding line and drop them through the loop as shown in illustration 1, then pull it tight as shown in illustration 2.

Lark's Head

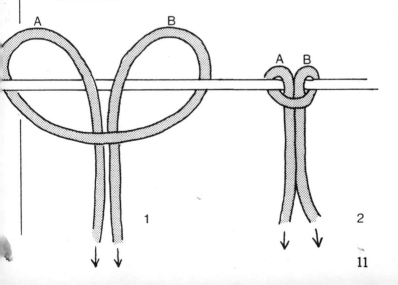

1

2

11

2. Double Clove Hitch with Picot — This knot is also worked in a series around a holding line. It is preferred over the Lark's Head when it is important that a certain width be maintained, or when the work is to remain on the holding line which will then be sewn or otherwise affixed to a skirt, shawl or poncho. It then becomes a border for the trimming.

To do the knot, slip a Lark's Head (Knot 1) *backwards* around the holding line, then lift the strand ends up and over on each side of the line and drop them inside the individual loops formed, see illustration 1. Pull the knot tightly, with the center loop at the top, to form the Picot, as shown in illustration 2.

Double Clove Hitch with Picot

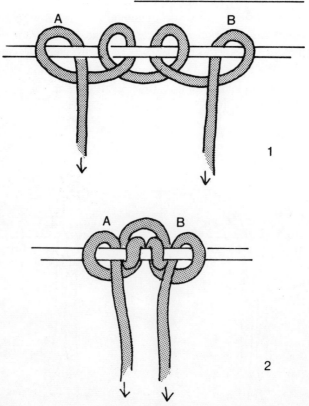

Basic Single Knots

3. Half Hitch — A simple turn used in chains and braids, a Half Hitch can be worked either from the left or right. The important thing to remember is that the tying cord should always pass *over* the anchor line. If you alternate you are doing a Lark's Head Braid (Knot 7).

4. Clove Hitch — This knot is actually two Half Hitches (Knot 3). Any piece that must be strong can be made so by a series of Clove Hitches. It also helps to stiffen the edges of your work.

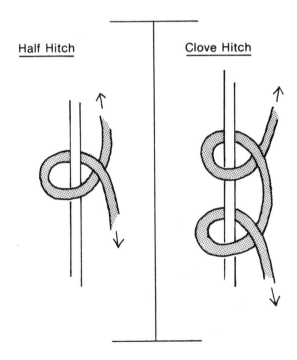

Half Hitch

Clove Hitch

5. Square Knot (Version 1) — Though it may look complicated, this knot is really quite a simple one to learn. To work it you need four strands, but if you look closely at the illustrations below you will notice that

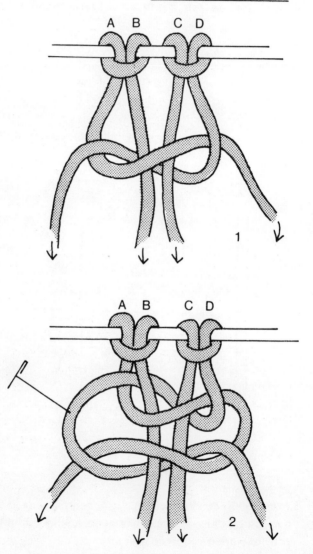

A   B   C   D

1

A   B   C   D

2

14

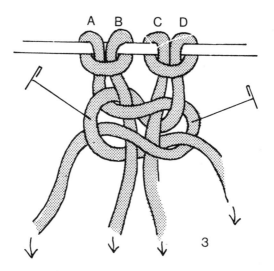

you work only the two outside strands. The two inner (anchor) strands are virtually ignored.

To start, place strand D under C and B and hold. Bring A under D, up *over* B and C, and through the loop at the right, as shown in illustration 1. Pull up. Following illustration 2, place A over C and B and hold. Bring D over A, up *under* B and C, and through the loop at the right. Pull up as shown in illustration 3.

To make a lovely bell or window shade pull, continue the steps to the desired length.

5. Square Knot (Version 2) — This version can be worked in place of Version 1. It is more complicated, but preferred when the working strands are long and are not bundled.

As shown in illustration 1, loop strand A over B and

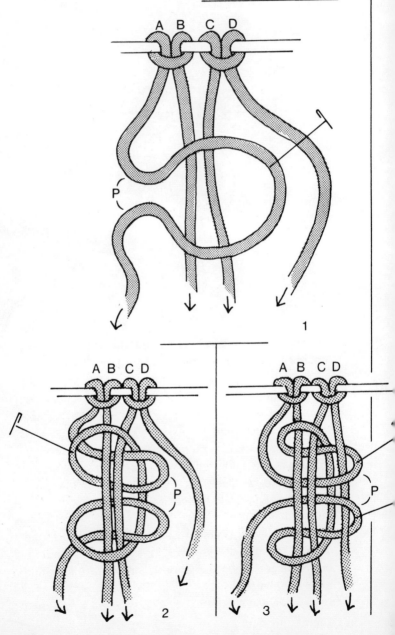

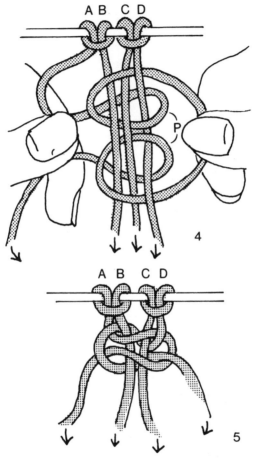

C, and grasp A at points P. Pull both points P
underneath strands B and C and *over* the single loop
formed by strand A, see illustration 2. Next, still
holding loops P, run strand D in and out of the loops
as shown in illustration 3. Following illustration 4, hold
strands, pull initial single loop outward, as shown, and
release. Pulling down, straighten strand ends then
tighten and pull up first the top half and then the
bottom half of the knot to complete.

6. Overhand Knot — This is a great utility knot which is also used decoratively either in a series or alone. It is often tied at the ends of cords to prevent fraying. To position the knot, make the knot loosely in the general area, insert a T-pin or milliner's pin in the knotting board at the exact position you want the knot, and tighten the cord around it. Remove the pin, and your knot is in position.

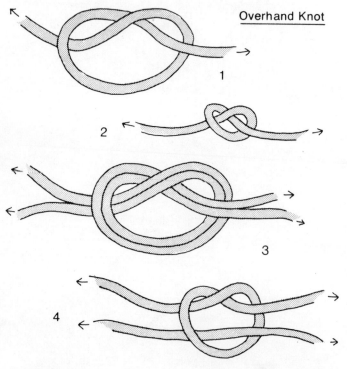

Overhand Knot

Illustration 1 shows the Overhand Knot being executed with 1 strand and illustration 2 shows it tightened. Illustration 3 shows the exact same knot, but this time it is executed with 2 strands. This knot can be worked with any number of strands, and is often used at the end of a chain or braid forming a belt to keep the knots in place. In illustration 4, a strand is shown worked around an anchor cord.

Basic Chains and Braids

7. Lark's Head Braid — For this braid, what you are essentially doing is using one strand as an anchor or holding cord and placing a series of Lark's Heads (Knot 1) on it. However, since one end of the tying cord is fastened, the knot must be done differently than as explained earlier ... it 'is, however, just as easy. As shown in the diagram, strand A remains straight, while strand B is brought down, *over* strand A, up the back and forward through the loop to complete half the knot. Then strand B is again brought

Lark's Head Braid

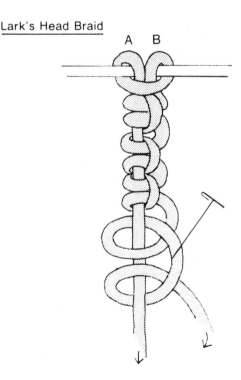

down, *under* strand A, up the front and backward through the loop to complete the entire Lark's Head. Repeat the knot to make a braid.

8. Alternating Lark's Head Braid — Using strand A as a tying cord, tie one Lark's Head — according to the special instructions for the Lark's Head Braid (Knot 7) — around strands B and C. Next use strand D to tie a Lark's Head around strands C and B, directly under the first Lark's Head. Repeat the above directions alternating right and left outer strands.

This design, used in strips for an added effect, is perfect for sashes or room dividers.

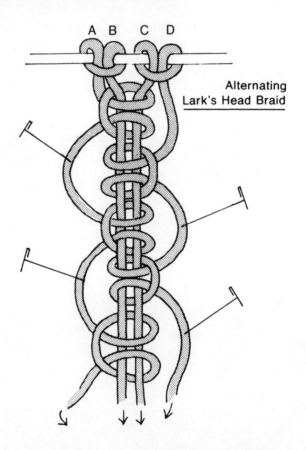

A   B   C   D

Alternating
Lark's Head Braid

9. Double Alternating Lark's Head Braid — With this design, it is necessary to have eight strands. Strands B and C and strands F and G are anchor cords while

20

A and D and E and H are tying (working) cords. With strand A, tie a special Lark's Head (Knot 7) around B and C. With strand H, tie a Lark's Head around F and G. With D, tie a Lark's Head around F and G. With E, tie a Lark's Head around B and C. Repeat the above, always remembering to cross strand E *over* strand D.

Double Alternating Lark's Head Braid

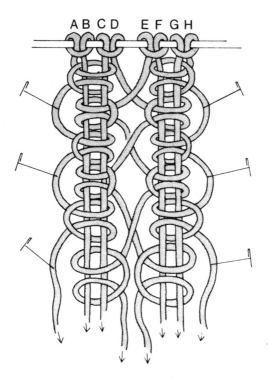

A B C D   E F G H

This design can be made to any width providing there is a multiple of four strands — 12, 16, 20, etc. — and the central loops can be linked or bound together with blending or contrasting cord or yarn.

We have used this braid in our projects section to make a lovely headband and belt set.

10. Half Hitch Braid — Using one strand as a tying cord, tie as many Half Hitches (Knot 3) as needed around the other strand or anchor cord. This braid can be kept flat or, if you so desire, it will twist very attractively.

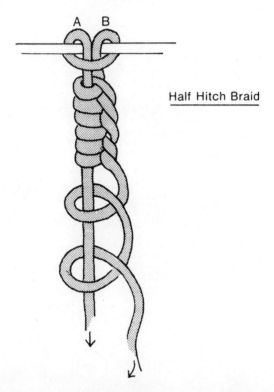

Half Hitch Braid

The Half Hitch Braid can be used for making narrow belts, purse handles, dog leads, necklaces, bracelets, and many other such items. It may also be tied around wide leather belts as an added trim.

11. Alternating Half Hitch Braid — Here you work with four strands of cord, using first strand A and then strand D as a tying cord. With strand A, tie a Half Hitch (Knot 3) around B and C. Next, Half Hitch strand D around C and B. Repeat the above, alternating strands A and D and continuing until you reach the desired length.

This braid alone makes a lovely belt or sash, although colorful beads may add interest.

Alternating Half Hitch Braid

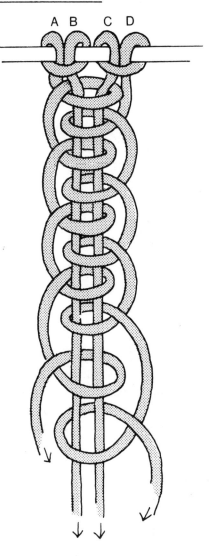

A B   C D

12. Triple Half Hitch Braid — This unusual-looking braid is quite easy to make. Using strand A as a tying cord, simply make a Half Hitch (Knot 3) around strand B, then around strands B and C, and then around strand B again. Using strand D, make a Half Hitch around strand C, around strands C and B, and then around strand C again. Repeat this procedure alternating strands A and D to the desired length.

This braid, in addition to the Alternating Half Hitch Braid, is a beautiful trim for a bolero, jacket or boot tops.

Triple Half Hitch Braid

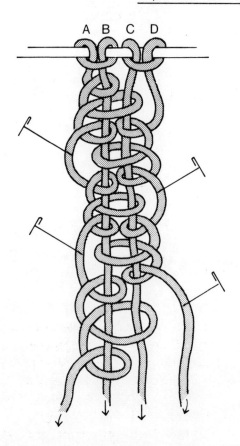

13. Alternating Half Hitch Chain — This chain is formed by having two strands alternate as tying and anchor cords. First strand A is Half Hitched (Knot 3) onto strand B, then strand B is Half Hitched onto strand A. Repeat, alternating knots to the desired length.

The fact that this chain is very flexible makes it perfect for all kinds of trimming — sleeves, collars, lamp shades, etc.

Alternating Half Hitch Chain

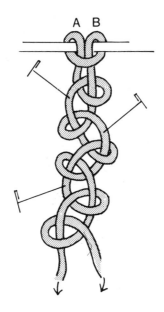

14. Two Strand Alternating Half Hitch Chain — This chain is worked the same as the regular Alternating Half Hitch Chain (Knot 13), except that here you use four strands, and Half Hitch two strands together. Even more bulk can be added by using 6 or 8 strands and Half Hitching 3 or 4 strands together.

No matter how many strands are used, this very

Two Strand Alternating Half Hitch Chain

decorative chain remains flexible and easy to work with. It can be used either plain or with beads added at intervals to make a comfortable, attractive necklace (see our Bead-A-Link Necklace in the project section of this book), or a belt with fancy ends for ties. It is also a perfect chain to experiment with in terms of color — blue and green, orange and yellow, red and purple, gray and gold — there are many intriguing possibilities.

15. Horizontal Clove Hitch — To do this hitch, you need another strand fastened for use as a horizontal anchor cord. Tie an Overhand Knot (Knot 6) in the end of the cord and place the strand directly below

Horizontal Clove Hitch

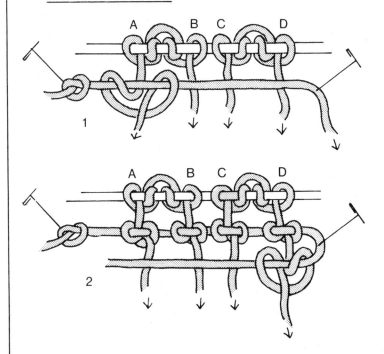

and parallel to the holding cord. Fasten the knot to the board to the right of the work. Pull the line taut and then pin or otherwise fasten it at the other side of the work to keep it in place, but *do not cut*. Following illustration 1, use strand A to tie a Clove Hitch (a variation of Knot 4) around the anchor cord and pull it tight. Continue on to strand B, C and D and Clove Hitch each strand to the anchor cord. As shown in illustration 2, pick up the loose end of the anchor cord, stretch it back across the four strands and refasten. Clove Hitch the row, using strands D, C, B and A, and reposition the anchor cord. Continue on to the desired length of the piece.

With this hitch, the area that you wish to be knotted can be made as wide as needed, simply add more Double Clove Hitches with Picot (Knot 2) to the holding line.

Used in sections, with beads, this stitch forms a lovely, interesting wall hanging.

16. Vertical Clove Hitch — This hitch is worked pretty much the same as the Horizontal Clove Hitch (Knot 15) *except* that the anchor cord now becomes the tying cord. Following illustration 1, anchor the new strand off one end of the work and use it to Clove Hitch each strand separately. Then pin, as shown in illustration 2 and reverse direction, Clove Hitching each strand you come to in order.

Vertical Clove Hitch

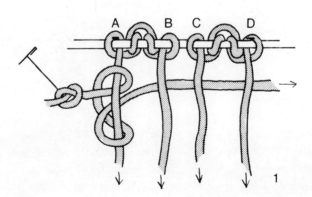

1

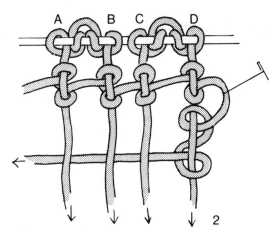

Like the Horizontal Clove Hitch, this stitch makes a very effective wall hanging, especially when a different color cord is introduced.

17. Diagonal Clove Hitch — Here, the first row is worked exactly like the Horizontal Clove Hitch (Knot 15), but when the added anchor cord is turned for the second row it is placed across the strands and hitches are placed on it *diagonally*. It is very important that the anchor line be held taut at all times and that each hitch is tightened as you go along.

Use this design to make a lovely multicolor sash, or bell pull.

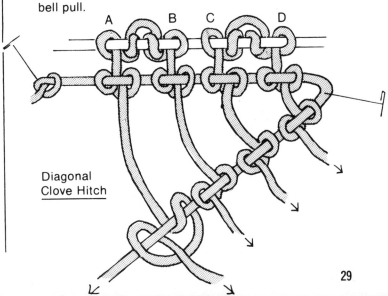

Diagonal
Clove Hitch

29

18. Double Diagonal Clove Hitch — This is simply an extension of the Diagonal Clove Hitch (Knot 17) preceding. For the second diagonal row, use strand D of the previous row as the anchor cord, stretch it across strands C, B and A and the *old* anchor cord and tie Clove Hitches around it. The last Clove Hitch of this row is, therefore, tied with the anchor cord of the previous row. Tighten each knot as it is tied.

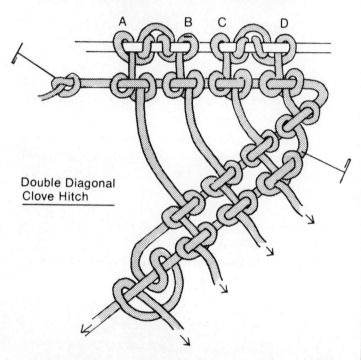

Double Diagonal
Clove Hitch

19. Chevron Clove Hitch — This knot may be worked with any multiple of 2 strands, although our instructions and diagrams use 8 strands. Following illustration 1, use strands B, C and D to tie Clove Hitches around anchor cord A, being sure to keep cord A *at an angle*. Use strand G to tie a Clove Hitch around anchor cord H. Next, use strands F and E to tie Clove Hitches around anchor cord H, as shown in illustration 2. In order to finish the center, tie H in a Clove

Hitch around anchor cord A. Then, as in illustration 3, tie C, D and H around anchor cord B and tie strand F around anchor cord G. Following illustration 3, use strands E and A to tie Clove Hitches around G. And, in order to finish the center, use B to tie a Clove Hitch around G.

Chevron Clove Hitch

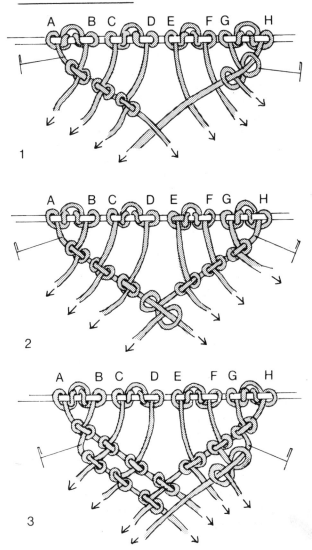

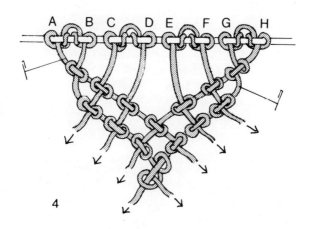

A B C D E F G H

4

When planning a large piece which will combine different textures and different knotting patterns, such as in a wall hanging or a room divider, this hitch should definitely be considered. It is really lovely and impressive.

20. Alternating Clove Hitch Braid — This knot uses four strands of cord, or whatever material desired. With strand A, tie a Clove Hitch (Knot 4) around anchor cords B and C. Next, use strand D to tie a Clove Hitch around C and B. Repeat the above directions, alternating strands A and D as tying cords.

This braid can be used to make a belt, dog lead, or handles for a purse or bag.

Alternating Clove Hitch Braid

A B C D

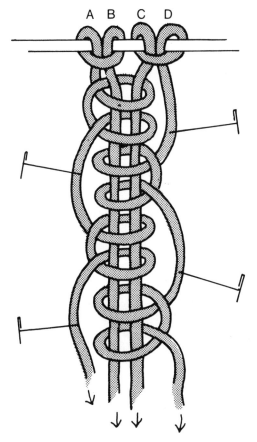

21. Square Knot Braid — This braid is simply a series of Square Knots (Knot 5). As shown in illustration 1, strands A and D are used to tie a series of Square

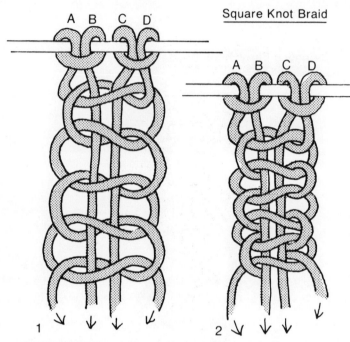

Square Knot Braid

A B C D

A B C D

1

2

Knots loosely around anchor cords B and C. Illustration 2 shows the end result after the knots are tightened.

The closeness of this braid makes it perfect for use in making twine placemats or hotplate mats, or as a bag base. But don't overlook the possibility of using heavy nylon cord or leather laces to make a tie belt. Try it and see.

22. Two Strand Square Knot Braid — In order to do this knot you must have eight strands, and work with them in pairs. Use strands A and B, and G and H in pairs to tie a series of Square Knots (Knot 5) around the anchor cords C, D, E, and F.

Two Strand Square Knot Braid

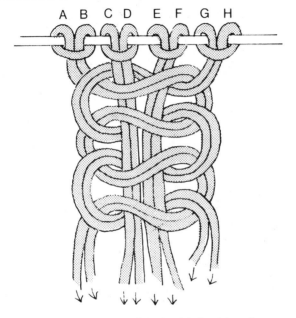

A B   C D   E   F G H

Combining various colors in this braid makes a very beautiful design for use in a placemat or a rug square.

23. Spiral Half Square Knot Braid — This is a very interesting braid that automatically spirals around its anchor cords as it is worked. To tie a Half Square Knot, place strand D under C and B and bring A under D, then over B and C, and through the loop formed, as shown in illustration 1. If this procedure sounds familiar to you, it should be. It is simply the first half of the regular Square Knot (Knot 5) Version 1. (You cannot make *half* a Square Knot using Version 2.) With the same strands, tie five more Half Square Knots and, as you can see in illustration 2, the sixth

Half Square Knot completes one spiral. To do this braid correctly, however, it is important to remember always to keep cords D and A going in the same direction.

Spiral Half Square Knot Braid

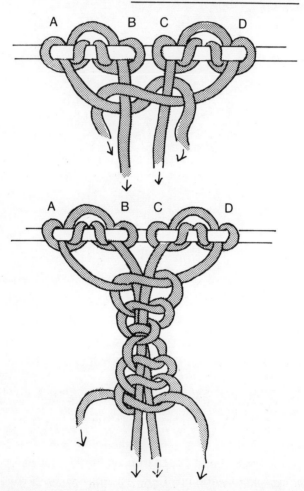

This design makes a very effective tie belt, especially if you use handspun wool since that gives the design a very open work look.

Also, see the Beaded Yarn Necklace in our projects section.

24. Looped Square Knot Braid — Here you work with four strands of cord in much the same way as the Square Knot Braid (Knot 21), but you form loops on the outer edges by hooking the tying cords around dowels, pencils or T-pins between knots as shown.

Looped Square Knot Braid

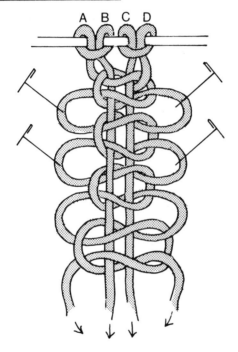

This design can be used in conjunction with other intricate patterns to form a beautiful wall hanging or room divider.

25. Knotted and Looped Square Knot Braid — This braid is worked just the same as the Looped Square Knot Braid (Knot 24) except that, using the two anchor cords, you tie a Double Overhand Knot (Knot 6) between each pair of Looped Square Knots, as shown.

Knotted and Looped Square Knot Braid

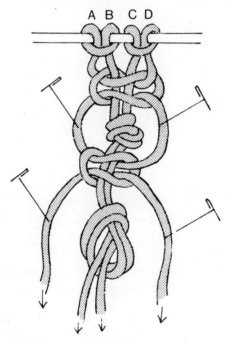

This braid can be used in strips, with the loops linked together, for a very beautiful room divider or window shade.

26. Knotted Loop Square Knot Braid — This braid is worked almost the same as the Looped Square Knot Braid (Knot 24) except that you tie an Overhand Knot (Knot 6) in each loop of strands A and D before making the next Square Knot.

This braid and the Looped Square Knot Braid can be worked together in strips to make window curtains or a room divider. Instead of merely *linking* the loops together to form wide fabrics, do a variation of the

Knotted Loop Square Knot Braid

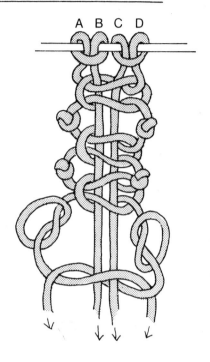

Overhand Knot (Knot 6, illustration 4) knotting each loop in this braid to a neighboring (knotless) loop of the Looped Square Knot Braid.

27. Beaded Knot Braid — Starting with four strands, use strands A and D to make a Square Knot (Knot 5) around anchor cords B and C. Leave an opening the size of one knot, see illustration, and tie three more Square Knots. Next, bring the anchor cords up, through the opening and down. Pull the cords tight, as shown in illustration 3, to form a bead on top. Then use strands A and D to tie a Square Knot *below* the bead, as in illustration 4.

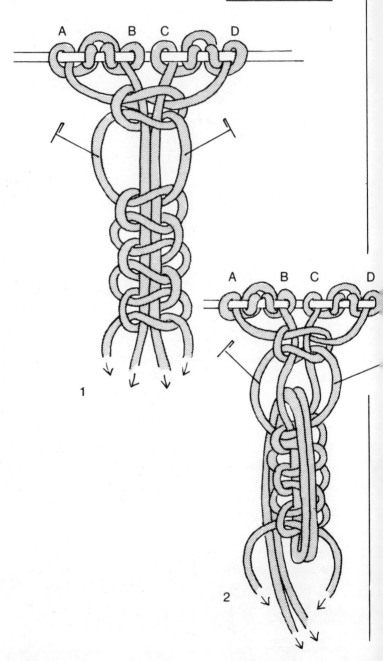

A B C D

1

A B C D

2

40

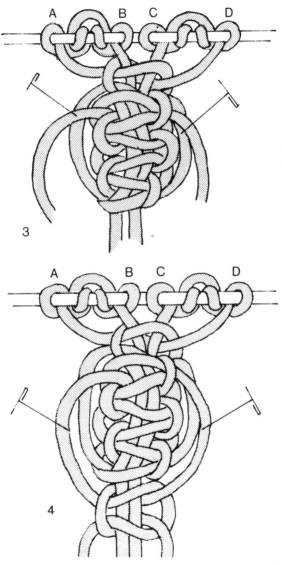

To enlarge the size of the bead, simply increase the number of Square Knots made after the opening. Five, six or more Square Knots, and the bead becomes a ring.

28. Alternating Square Knot — The following diagram shows this design being worked with twelve strands. To do it properly, you must have at least eight strands, and may have any multiple of four strands. For the first row, use strands A and D to tie a Square Knot (Knot 5) around B and C, and knot strands E and H around F and G, and strands I and L around J and K.

Alternating Square Knot

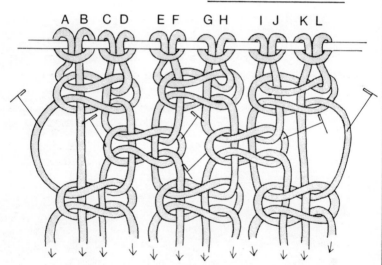

For the second row, knot strands C and F around D and E, and then G and J around H and I. (If desired, Overhand Knots may be centered in the loops formed by strands A and L, or those strands may be Half Hitched around anchor strands B and K, rather than leaving the loops free as shown in the illustration above. Repeat the first and second rows to the length desired. Always be sure, however, that strands B and K remain anchor cords throughout.

This design can be used to make a multi-colored room divider . . . or, using heavy but soft yarn, a stole! As a cushion cover, it can turn a slightly faded or discolored cushion into a lovely conversation piece.

Ornamental Knots

29. Monkey's Fist — Following the six diagrams below, wind the cord around your fingers several times. Then, wrap the cord or material used around the original windings an equal number of times. When you are finished wrapping, string the cord inside and through, as shown in illustration 3. Slide the cord off the fingers and insert a smooth rock, bead or marble, about 1/2 inch diameter, into the open cage made by the wrappings, centering it as shown in illustration 4. While holding it in place, complete wrapping the last bit of cord around the centered ball. In order to

Monkey's Fist

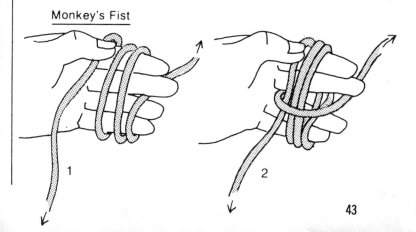

1   2

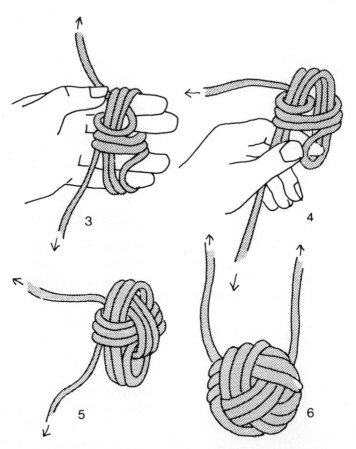

tighten the Monkey's Fist just where it is wanted on the cord, pull up and tighten each bit of cord into place until a firm covering has been made for the ball. There will be two cords extending from the finished knot and, if you have no use for them, cut them short and work the ends under the wrapping. Glue securely.

This knot may be used to decorate the ends of a design, such as a wall hanging.

30. Turk's Head Knot — This knot is also worked with only one strand of your working material. Following the eight diagrams below, hold one end of the cord with your thumb and wind the cord twice around your fingers. Then turn your hand and, still holding onto the starting end of the cord, weave the other end under the right loop, as shown in illustration 2. Next, bring the left cord over the right and weave the cord through the opening. Then weave the cord in and out as shown in illustrations 6 and 7. This completes the

Turk's Head Knot

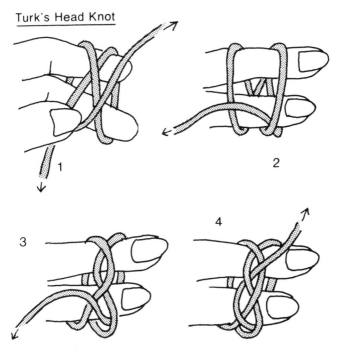

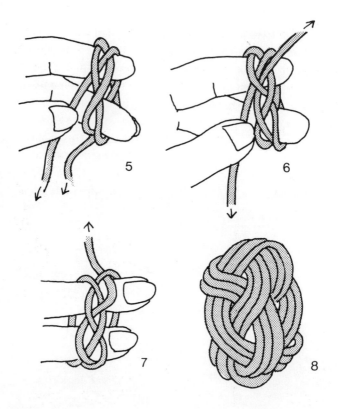

5

6

7

8

basic wrapping. With the cord, continue following the previous weaving pattern to complete the three strand Turk's Head as shown in illustration 8. Tighten the cord and cut, then glue the ends inside.

This knot is very decorative and provides a very intriguing finishing touch to any piece. The knot may also be worked in leather and suspended from a chain as a pendant.

31. Flattened Turk's Head Knot — This is a very ornamental knot that again uses just one strand. To begin, follow illustrations 1 through 7 of the Turk's Head Knot (Knot 30) then slide the work from your

Flattened Turk's
Head Knot

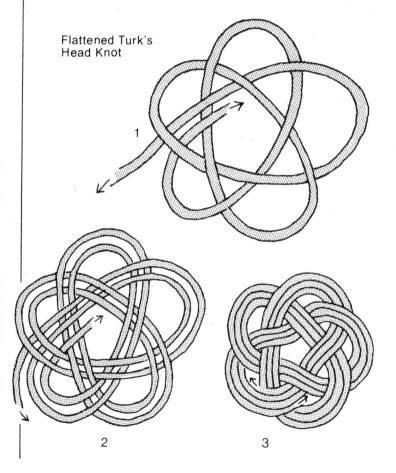

1

2

3

hand and flatten it out, as shown in illustration 1 (p. 47). Then continue weaving the working strand, following the previous weaving, until the knot has three strands. You can now cut the cord or string and glue the ends to the underside.

This knot may be worked with string or a lightweight cord, or a heavy or decorative type cord to be used as trim on clothing or accessories. A leather strip woven just once makes a beautiful ring decoration (see back cover). There are many more uses for this knot. It is well worth a little extra effort.

32. Oriental Knot — Use two strands of cord together to work this knot. Following illustration 1, hold both strands at the upper left, make two loops and pass the working cords through the first loop. Then bring the working cords up and *over* the strand ends. Continu-

Oriental Knot

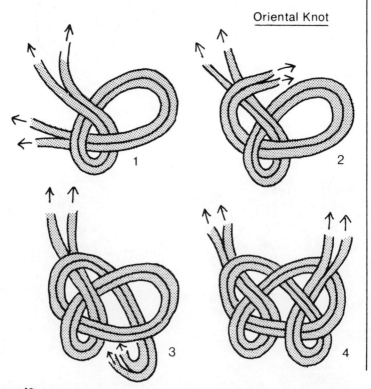

ing, bring the working cords down under the second loop, then weave cords through the knot, as shown in illustration 4. Tighten the knot.

This knot can be used on the ends of tie belts, instead of anchoring on, or as a trim to be sewn on a dress neckline.

33. Oriental Knot II — Here again you use two strands of cord together. Make two loops as shown in illustration 1, holding the starting ends at the upper left. Weave the working cords through the knot, following the diagrams, to complete the knot. Tighten the knot.

Oriental Knot II

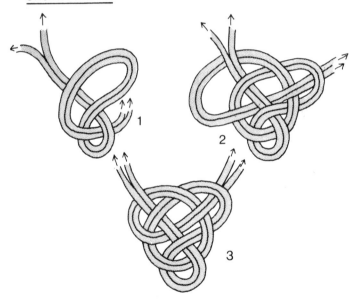

This knot is a lovely trim for a neckline, the front and back corners of a poncho, or for accessories. Using heavy decorative cord, this knot alone makes a lovely necklace. Simply center the knot on the cords, and tie at the back.

34. Josephine Knot — The Josephine Knot is worked with two strands of material on an anchor cord. Following illustration 1, make a loop with strand A being sure the lower part of the strand is *under* the upper part, and lay strand B over the top of it. As shown in illustration 2, bring strand B around under the leg of the loop and over strand A. Continue weaving strand B through the knot as shown, in and out of the loop, thus completing the first knot.

Josephine Knot

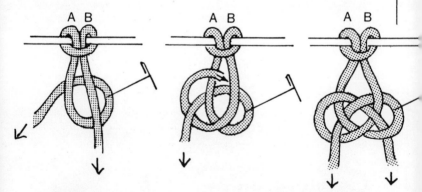

Following illustration 4, loop strand A again to the right, but the *reverse* of the loop in illustration 1, with strand B passing, this time, *under* the loop. Complete the second knot as shown. Continue in the same order, repeating pairs of knots.

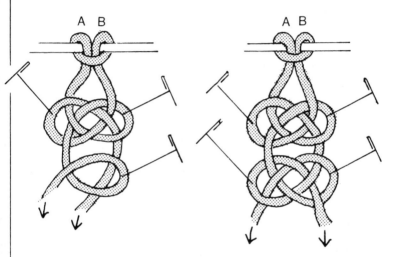

This braid alone makes a very beautiful belt design, especially when heavy decorative, possibly metallic, cord is used. It can also be used to make a headband, bracelet, dog collar, or ring. A ring made with light twine or string may be given a little body by wetting throughly with spray starch and letting dry.

Finishing Knot

35. Cinch Knot — This knot is worked like the Square Knot (Knot 5) except that it is tied with any number of strands around any number of anchor cords. (The diagram on the next page shows two pairs of strands tied around six anchor cords.)

This knot is used to gather strands together to make sections of thick fringe or tassels, and is sometimes used in conjunction with Overhand Knots (Knot 6) to secure a finished piece of work. It is a very effective way to finish off a wall hanging.

Cinch Knot

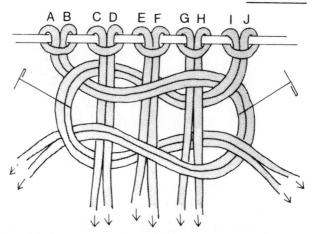

A B   C D   E F   G H   I J

Some Things to Make

Following are a sampling of macramé projects (from simple to medium, none truly difficult) to give you a taste of the art of macramé. Try them, altering where necessary to suit your own needs and desires. The Beaded Leather Sleeve Trim, the Bead-A-Link Necklace and the Square Knot Belt are quite easy to do. The Tricolored Belt, the Fantasy Hanging, and the

Macramé Tote Bag are the hardest. In between you will find the Quick Choker Necklace, the Hanging Plant Basket, the Beaded Band and Belt Set, the Looped Tie Belt, and the Beaded Yarn Necklace . . . so get out your knotting board, pick your first project, and Lark's Head (Knot 1) on.

Easy Bead-A-Link Necklace

MATERIALS

12 yards of heavy cord or yarn, your choice of color
36 beads, 1/2 inch in diameter

Step 1: Cut the cord into 2 lengths of 6 yards each, find the center and Lark's Head (Knot 1) the cords onto a holding line. Taking 24 beads, string 12 onto strands A and B together, and strands C and D together (these strands will be worked in pairs), then bundle each pair of strands for easy handling.

Step 2: Drop down about 6 inches, then work the two strand Alternating Half-Hitch Chain (Knot 14). Push a bead up into the work each time a pair of strands is used as the tying cord, just *before* they are used as the anchor cord. If you keep this rule in mind you will be alternating beads correctly. Note, too, that beads should *not* be side-by-side, see the illustration below. Try to space the knots about 1 inch apart. Continue until you reach the desired length or until you have only about 6 inches of unknotted cord left.

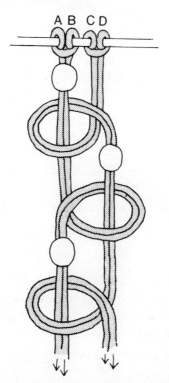

Step 3: If you have not used up all the beads strung earlier, release them. Cut the Lark's Head loops holding the necklace to the holding line taking care that no knots unravel. Bring the two ends of the necklace together and tie an Overhand Knot (Knot 6) using all 8 strands.

Step 4: Trim ends to a uniform length (if desired) and string a bead onto each strand. Tie an Overhand Knot in each strand about an inch from the end and pull the bead down and in place over it. (Note: if the diameter of the bead is too large to fit snugly over the knotted strand of cord selected simply add some white glue to the Overhand Knot before bringing the bead down over it. Let dry.)

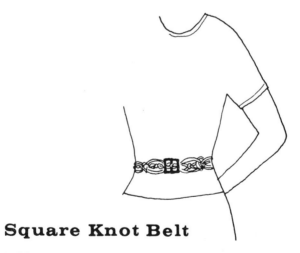

Square Knot Belt

SIZE

Waist size plus 6 inches

MATERIALS

Heavy cord or twine 8 times the waist size plus 6 inches (for instance, 24" + 6" = 30" X 8 = 240 inches or 20 feet)

Slide buckle (no center prong)

DIRECTIONS

Step 1: Pin or otherwise affix the slide buckle to the top of the knotting board face side up. Cut the cord into 2 equal lengths, fold them in half and use a Lark's Head (Knot 1), or a Double Clove Hitch with Picot (Knot 2) if the buckle is a wide one, to anchor the cords to the center rod of the buckle, see illustration below. Bundle each of the four strands for easy handling.

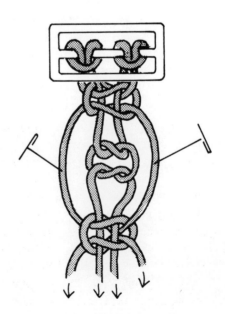

Step 2: Use strands A and D to tie a Square Knot (Knot 5) around anchor cords B and C.

Step 3: Use strands B and C to tie a Reef Knot without anchor cords. (Follow the diagram for the route of the two strands in working the Reef Knot.)

Step 4: Repeat Steps 2 and 3 to reach the length desired, ending with a Square Knot.

Step 5: To finish off, tie Reef Knots as tightly as possible with strands A and D and strands B and C. Then tie another Reef Knot with strands B and C. Leaving about 1/2 inch, cut off remainder of cord. Turn raw edges, use a needle to weave them into the underside of the work and glue.

Note: A tie belt can be easily made by allowing for the additional length (using more twine or cord) and by anchoring on to a holding line rather than a buckle. Also, to give the tie belt a tattered-fringe effect, tie an Overhand Knot (Knot 6), using all 4 strands, about 3 or 4 inches from the end of the belt and deliberately unravel the ends. Sisal twine unravels well, but some cords do not unravel readily. In this case, you may end the belt by tying Overhand Knots spaced an inch or so apart in each cord. Or, if the strand ends are long enough, you may finish off each strand with a Monkey's Fist (Knot 29) or Turk's Head Knot (Knot 30).

Beaded Leather Sleeve Trim

MATERIALS

24 two-foot long leather thongs (16 yards)

144 wooden or natural color beads

Step 1: Measure the sleeves and mark 12 places, spaced equally apart, on each sleeve to receive the thongs. *Recheck* your measurements. Find the center of the thongs and punch or otherwise work them through the sleeve material, preferably on either side of the sleeve's seam. Be sure, first, that the material is *not* the kind that will unravel. Lark's Head (Knot 1) the thongs to the sleeves.

Step 2: Take thong A and string on a bead, tie an Overhand Knot (Knot 6) below the bead 3 inches from the top. Add a second bead, and tie another Overhand Knot 3 inches below the first. Add a third bead and tie another Overhand Knot 3 inches below the last. Let the last 3 inches of thong hang free.

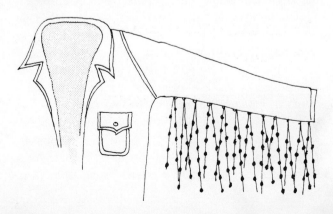

Step 3: With thong B (the other half of the same cord), string on a bead and drop down 4 1/2 inches before tying the first Overhand Knot. Then space the following knots 3 inches apart. In this way the beads and knots will alternate with thong A.

Step 4: Continue, working Steps 2 and 3, with every other thong.

Hanging Plant Basket

MATERIALS

1 ball of medium weight twine
1 6-foot length of knitting or rug yarn
16 to 32 feet of brightly colored yarn scraps, each about 1 foot in length
24 3/8-inch diameter beads
Beading wire
White glue

Step 1: Cut twelve 2 1/2 (3 or 3 1/2) yard lengths of twine, depending on the size of the pot to be suspended. Using 3 strands each, make 4 flat braids and secure both ends of each braid with beading wire. Hold the 4 completed braids together, fold in half, then secure ends together with beading wire about 3 inches from the cut ends — this is the bottom of the basket.

Step 2: Suspend the secured bottom of the basket upward, possibly from a chair-rail or doorknob, and cross 2 adjacent braids (one over the other) about 1 1/2 inches below the beading wire. Wind a 1 foot length of yarn tightly around the 2 braids where they cross. Repeat this process 3 more times around the basket to complete the first row.

Step 3: Re-divide the braids, cross them again 2 1/2 to 3 inches below the first row. Repeat the winding process around the basket to produce a diamond-shaped pattern, see illustration 1. The size of the flowerpot will determine the number of times it is necessary to divide the braids in order to hold the pot securely. The pattern should come up to the top edge of the flowerpot. You will probably find it necessary to divide the braids 3 or 4 times to fit a 4 to 6 inch diameter flowerpot.

Step 4: Then, continue winding the same 2 braids together every 4 inches, no longer producing the diamond-shaped pattern, to decorate and strengthen the braids. When you come to within 6 inches of the center fold of the 4 tied sections, secure all together with beading wire.

Step 5: Turn basket right side up, the 4-braid loop on top. Fold the 6 yard length of yarn in half then tie a series of Half Hitches (Knot 3) around the loop above the beading wire until the braid is completely covered, see illustration 2. Tuck the ends of the yarn under the beading wire. Wind a piece of yarn around this beading wire and another piece around the beading wire at the bottom of the basket to conceal it.

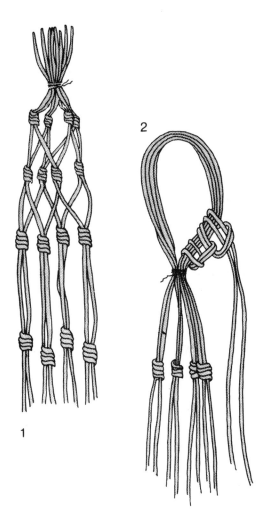

1

2

Step 6: If desired, a bead trim can be added to the bottom fringe. Dip the ends of the twine into white glue, then insert them into the holes in the beads (a needle or pin may be helpful here) and let dry.

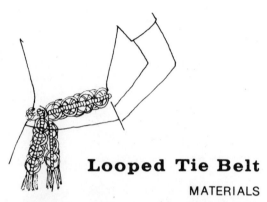

Looped Tie Belt

MATERIALS

Four cords of equal length, 8 times the proposed length of the finished belt

DIRECTIONS

Step 1: Halve the cords and, using the Lark's Head (Knot 1), tie the cords to the holding line. If the strands are very long, bundle each one separately and fasten them with rubber bands. Start knotting about three inches down from the holding line.

Step 2: Following the illustration (p.63), use strand B to tie a Lark's Head around anchor cords C, D, E and F. (These strands remain anchor cords throughout.)

Step 3: Use strand G to tie a Lark's Head around the anchor cords.

Step 4: Use strand A to tie a Lark's Head around the anchor cords. Try to keep the loops as even as possible.

Step 5: Use strand H to tie a Lark's Head around the anchor cords. Push knots together tightly on anchor cords.

Step 6: Repeat Steps 2 to 5 for the length of the belt.

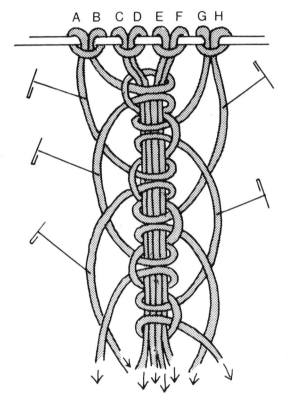

Step 7: Use strands A and B together and strands G and H together and tie a Cinch Knot (Knot 35). Then tie three Overhand Knots (Knot 6) using together strands A, B and C (2 tying and 1 anchor cord), D and E (2 anchor cords), and F, G and H (2 tying and 1 anchor cord). Push the knots up into place tightly and evenly, see illustration.

Step 8: Cut the loops of the Lark's Heads on the holding line. Repeat Step 7 with this end of the belt.

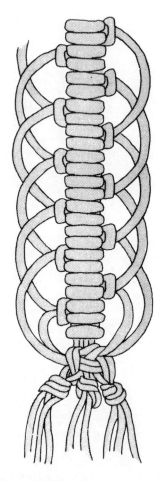

Step 9: Trim both ends of the belt evenly and let unknotted ends hang free.

Note: Variations of this pattern can be made by placing Overhand Knots in the loops, by adding beads loosely in the loops (onto strands A, B, G and H), or by using them in combination so that the Overhand Knots hold the beads in place.

Quick Choker Necklace

MATERIALS

32 feet of macramé cord or twine

DIRECTIONS .

Step 1: Cut 4 lengths of cord, 2 five feet long and 2 three feet long, and tie them together with an Overhand Knot (Knot 6) approximately 6 inches from the ends. Fasten the knot to the top of the knotting board or slip it into a drawer and spread out the strands with the 2 shorter ones in the center. These are the anchor cords.

Step 2: Work the Square Knot Braid (Knot 21) until you have enough braid to go around your neck (usually about 12 inches of braid).

Step 3: Tie an Overhand Knot using all four strands close to the braid. Remove the collar from the knotting board or drawer and tie Overhand Knots in each of the eight strands, about 1/2 inch from the ends, or tip with beads. The necklace may be worn now as a dog collar. But, if a hanging front is desired, . . .

Step 4: Cut 5 lengths of cord, 3 four feet long and 2 two feet long, and Lark's Head (Knot 1) them to the five central knots of the choker, the longer cords in the center.

Step 5: (ROW 1) Using strands A and C, tie 2 Square Knots around strand B. Using strands D and G, tie 2 Square Knots around strands E and F. Tie strands H and J around I.

Step 6: (ROW 2) Place strands A and J aside (they will be located on the outer edges of the work) then continue the pattern tying 2 Square Knots around strands C and D using B and E as working cords, and around strands G and H using F and I as working cords.

Step 7: Bring strands A and B together, and strands I and J together, and tie Overhand Knots. Let these strands hang loose.

Step 8: (ROW 3) Place strands C and H aside (these are now located on the outer edges of the work) then tie 2 Square Knots, using strands D and G, around E and F. Tie C and D together and H and G together with Overhand Knots, as in Step 6. Tie anchor cords E and F together with an Overhand Knot.

Step 9: Trim strands to the desired shape (V or U) and trim ends, if desired, with Overhand Knots or beads.

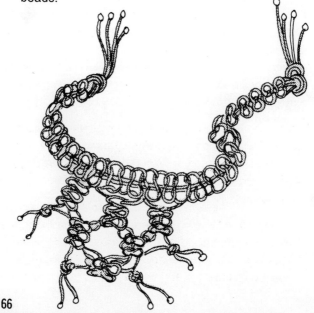

Beaded Band and Belt Set

MATERIALS

Cord or twine eight times the combined lengths of the
proposed belt and headband
Between 150 and 250 beads, depending on the length
of the pieces

DIRECTIONS

Step 1: Cut 4 lengths, each eight times as long as the
proposed piece — whether headband or belt. Find
the center and, using the Lark's Head (Knot 1),
anchor the cords to the holding line.

Step 2: If making a belt, add beads to strands A and
H, then bundle each strand separately to keep
them from tangling. Leave about 5 inches unknotted at the beginning, then start the Double
Alternating Lark's Head Braid (Knot 9). Push the

individual Lark's Heads up on the anchor cords as you do them. Slide the beads up into position when forming outer loops with strands A and H and try to keep the loops as uniform in size as possible, see illustration 1.

Step 3: Continue the braid until the pattern is long enough to go around your forehead, or until the belt reaches the length desired (approximately 54 to 60 inches for a tie belt). Then, using cords A and B, C and D, E and F, and G and H together *in pairs,* see illustration 2, tie Overhand Knots (Knot 6).

Step 4: Leave 5 inches of cord unknotted and trim off the excess.

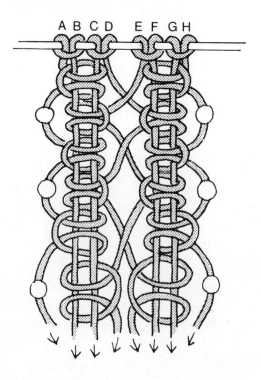

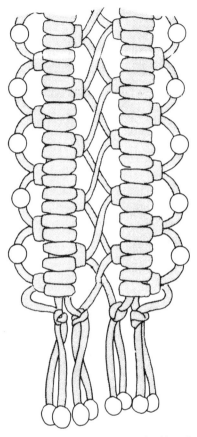

Step 5: Cut the loops of the Lark's Heads anchoring the work to the holding line and, using those strands in pairs, knot as described in Step 3, and finish off as in Step 4.

Note: For a headband, the loose strands are used for tying, on a belt they become fringe. If desired, additional beads can be placed on the ends of each strand or pair of strands. Simply dip the ends in white glue and use a needle to work them into the beads, then let dry.

Macramé Tote Bag

SIZE

Approximately 10 inches by 13 inches

MATERIALS

650 feet of 2-ply sisal twine
1 foot of heavy lining fabric, at least 27 inches wide
Matching thread
T-pins
Needle
40 Rubber bands

DIRECTIONS

Step 1: Measure and cut twenty 9 yard lengths of twine. (If you don't have a yardstick, you can easily measure off 9 yard lengths by wrapping the twine around a 12 inch piece of cardboard 14 1/2 times.) When this is finished, cut two strands of twine 7 feet long (wrap the twine around the cardboard 3 1/2 times).

Step 2: Fold one 7 foot long cord 4 times, make Overhand Knots (Knot 6) at each end, and pin it to the top of the knotting board as the holding cord. Find the center of each 9 yard cord and Lark's Head (Knot 1) on to the holding cord — you now have 40 tying strands. Bundle each strand separately for easy handling and to stop tangles, and fasten them with heavy duty rubber bands.

Step 3: The pattern is worked from left to right. Using strands A, B, C and D, tie 2 Square Knots (Knot 5). Repeat 9 more times, using 4 strands each, for a total of 10 pairs of knots across the top. Use T-pins

where necessary to keep the knots aligned both horizontally and vertically. Try to keep the knots as tight as possible while working.

Step 4: For the second row, begin by Half-Hitching (Knot 3) strand A around strand B 3 times, then tie pairs of Square Knots across the row, starting with strands C, D, E and F, to a total of 9. You will have 2 strands left at the end of this row. Half-Hitch the *last* strand onto the one before it 3 times, as you did with strands A and B.

Step 5: Repeat Steps 3 and 4 until the pattern reaches about 26 inches, but *ends with Step 4.*

Step 6: Take the second 7 foot long cord, fold it 4 times, Overhand Knot it at each end, and place it against the *bottom* of the work. Then Clove Hitch (Knot 4) each strand to it.

Step 7: Trim the 40 strands to about 1/2 to 3/4 inch and use a needle to work the ends into the backs of the knots, then glue. (Strands may be also *sewn* to the back of the knots with a matching or neutral color thread which will give extra strength and security before gluing.) Fold the bag right sides together and sew or knot the sides together tightly. Then turn the bag right side out.

Step 8: To make the strap, cut three lengths of twine each 30 feet long (10 yards) and Lark's Head them onto a short holding cord. Bundle each *pair* of strands for easy handling. Now work the Square Knot Braid (Knot 21) using 6 strands (the two cords at each side for tying and the two center cords being anchor cords) to give the strap the extra strength and width it needs. Continue the braid until you reach the desired length. Then sew or knot the strap to the two top corners of the bag, see drawing.

Step 9: Cut the lining material to the width and complete length (front and back) of the bag, being sure to allow an extra 3/4 of an inch all around for seams. Fold in half, the right sides together, and sew up the side seams. Turn the raw edges at the top of the lining and hem. With the wrong side of the lining outward, place the pocket inside the macramé bag and sew it to the twine around the top of the bag.

Beaded Yarn Necklace

MATERIALS
21 large beads, 3/4 inch diameter
33 yards of 4-ply knitting yarn
8 wire ties

DIRECTIONS

Step 1: Cut off one yard of yarn, and cut it into 3 one-foot lengths. Place them aside. Take the remaining 32 yards of yarn and cut them into 8 four-yard lengths. (Simply fold the cord in half 3 times and cut the loops at each end.)

Step 2: Tie Overhand Knots (Knot 6) about 4 inches in from the ends of the 8 strands of yarn and pin to the top of the knotting board. Take each of the four outer strands (A, B, G and H) and bundle them *separately.* Take the four inner cords (C, D, E and F), bundle them *together,* and secure with a wire tie.

Step 3: Tie 3 inches of Spiral Half Square Knot Braid (Knot 23) using strands A and B, and G and H together as tying cords around the four anchor cords. String a bead onto the eight strands (a blunt needle may be of some help in working the yarn through).

Step 4: Tie 1 inch of Spiral Half Square Knot Braid, then add another bead. (Note that 3 inches of braid are tied between each bead group, with 1 inch

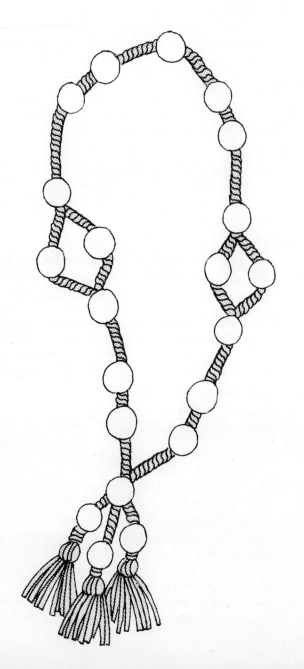

between each bead in the grouping. This may be altered, as you desire.)

Step 5: Repeat Step 3.

Step 6: To divide the necklace into two sections, as shown in the illustration, separate the 8 strands into two groups, each having two tying cords and two anchor cords. Tie 1 inch of Spiral Half Square Knot Braid with one grouping (now use *two* single strands to tie the braid around *two* anchor cords), add a bead and tie another inch of braid. Repeat the procedure with the other group.

Step 7: Bring the two groups together, add a bead, then continue tying the braid using all strands, as before. Continue to follow the pattern as illustrated.

Step 8: When the necklace has reached the desired length, tie the 8 cords from each side of the necklace together and add a bead. Divide the 16 cords into 3 groups (2 groups with 5 strands each and 1 group with 6 strands).

Step 9: Braid 2 inches of each group, using two strands of each group as tying cords, add a bead to each group, then braid another 1/2 inch.

Step 10: To make the tassels, cut a 4 inch piece of cardboard and wind the yarn around it about 40 times. Then cut the loops on one edge of the cardboard and tie the strands securely in the center, using one of the three unbraided ends of the necklace. Wind a 12 inch strand of yarn around the tassel, about 1/2 inch from the top. Work the end of the yarn into the windings. Trim the tassel evenly. Repeat for 2 more tassels.

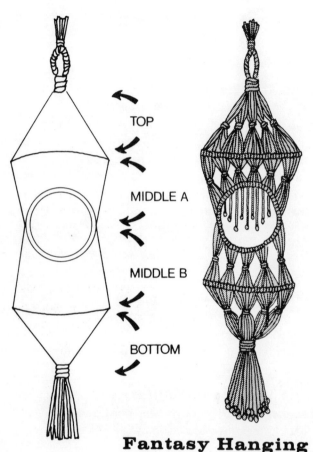

TOP

MIDDLE A

MIDDLE B

BOTTOM

Fantasy Hanging

MATERIALS

3 embroidery hoops, 5 inches in diameter

4 ounces of rug yarn in each of five colors

Possible color combinations:

RUST, YELLOW, ORANGE, BROWN, WHITE — PURPLE, LIGHT BLUE, DARK BLUE, BRIGHT GREEN, WHITE — ROSE, PINK, LILAC, PURPLE, WHITE

80 beads (color coordinated)
beading wire
blunt needle

DIRECTIONS

Step 1: Wrap each hoop in a different color yarn, completely covering the wood. Tuck in loose ends with a needle.

Step 2: Cut six 40-inch long strands of each of the five colors. Halve the strands and Lark's Head (Knot 1) each strand to one of the hoops using each color *in sequence*. (You now have 60 strands.)

Step 3: Place the hoop on end and, starting at the center of the strands, tie each strand, see illustration 1, around a horizontal hoop approximately 6 inches above — one strand going to one side of the

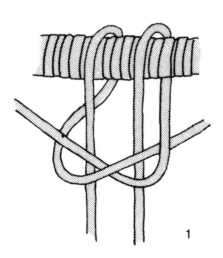

1

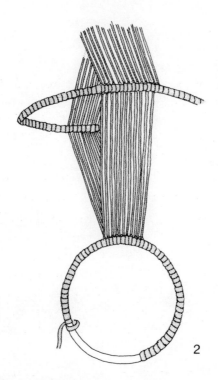

2

hoop and the second strand of the *same color* going to the *opposite* side of the hoop, see illustration 2. Continue until all the strands from the vertical hoop have been tied around the horizontal hoop. Gather the ends together and secure, for the moment, with a rubber band or wire tie.

Step 4: Repeat Step 2, this time covering the bottom half of the vertical hoop. (It might help here to suspend the hanging by the secured ends so that you can work on it more easily.)

Step 5: Repeat Step 3, tying each strand around a horizontal hoop approximately 8 inches *below* the vertical hoop.

Step 6: Release the strands at the top, straighten them and refasten tightly with beading wire, 5 inches above the uppermost horizontal hoop.

Step 7: Separate the strands into 2 groups and twist each group, then wire the groups together again to form a loop, as shown in illustration 3. Cover the beading wire with scraps of yarn and tuck the ends of the yarn into the work.

Step 8: Repeat Step 6 with the strands below the lower horizontal hoop. Let the strands hang free to form a tassel. Trim the tassel to a uniform length, as desired.

Step 9: The hanging is now divided into 4 parts, see illustration (p. 76), and the strands in each are to be divided differently. Divide the TOP into 10 groups of 6 strands each, tying each grouping in the middle with 8 inch scraps of the colors used in the hanging.

3

Step 10: Divide MIDDLE A into 12 groups of 5 strands each and fasten as in Step 9.

Step 11: Divide MIDDLE B ir.to 15 groups of 4 strands each and fasten.

Step 12: Divide the BOTTOM into 6 groups of 10 strands each and fasten.

Step 13: Trim *top* ends to about 1 1/2 inch in height and fluff. String beads onto tassel at *bottom* and tie Overhand Knots (Knot 6) near the end of each strand to secure the bead.

Step 14: To trim, fasten beads onto various short strands of yarn and suspend them inside the top or bottom horizontal hoops. Beads on various lengths of yarn may also be suspended in the center, vertical hoop, or this space may be used to display a favorite ornament.

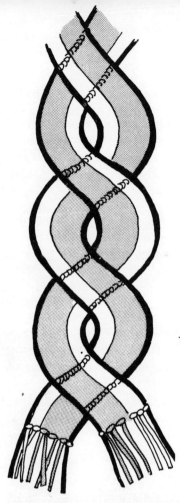

Tricolored Belt

LENGTH
54 inches (4 1/2 feet)

MATERIALS
31 yards of red and blue and 18 yards of white rug or cotton yarn

(Note: the amount of yarn needed is 3 times the desired length of the finished belt. Adjust for shorter or longer length belt.)

DIRECTIONS

Step 1: Cut the yarn into 4 1/2 yard lengths (six each red and blue cords and 4 white cords). Tie Overhand Knots (Knot 6) 5 inches from the ends of *pairs* of cords as follows: 2 red and white, 2 blue and white, 2 blue and blue, 2 red and red. Pin the knots in place at the top of the knotting board so that the strands fall in the following order:

A B C D E F G H I J K L M N O P
R W W B B B R R R R B B B W W R

Check the order to be certain that each strand falls into the proper color sequence, then bundle each cord for easy handling.

Step 2: Using the four red cords in the middle (G,H,I,J), tie a Square Knot (Knot 5). Place a pin in the knot to hold it securely.

Step 3: Taking red strand H, place it on top of the cords to the left of the center and hold it diagonally. Tie Diagonal Clove Hitches (Knot 17) onto strand H using each cord in succession. Pin knot-bearing strand H. off to the left of the work.

Step 4: Take up red strand I and place it diagonally on top of the cords to the right. Tie Diagonal Clove Hitches with each cord in succession, see illustration. Pin strand I to the knotting board at the right of the work.

Step 5: Except for strands H and I, grasp cords to the left of the center (A through G) in the left hand and the cords to the right of the center (J through P) in the right hand. Crisscross left-hand cords *over* right-hand cords so that each group runs in diagonal directions parallel to the rows of Diagonal Clove Hitches.

Step 6: Take the red knot-bearing cord (H) and place it diagonally *to the right* over the bottom group of cords and parallel to the top right row of Diagonal Clove Hitches. Tie Diagonal Clove Hitches using each of the bottom group of cords in succession.

Step 7: Take the red knot-bearing cord (I) and place it diagonally *to the left* over the top group of cords and parallel to the top left row of Diagonal Clove Hitches. Tie Diagonal Clove Hitches to strand I using each of the top group of cords in succession.

Step 8: With strands H and I now in the middle, tie 3 Overhand Knots (Knot 6). Pin them to hold them securely.

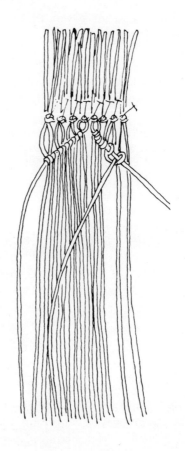

Step 9: Repeat Steps 3 through 8, leaving cords loose enough between repeats to make an arc to each side and form the design. Repeat until desired length is reached (the 56 inch long belt has about 14 repeats). Move the work up on the knotting board as your work progresses using as many pins as necessary. Keep the design as uniform as possible.

Step 10: End with a Square Knot, as in Step 2, then tie Overhand Knots in groups of two, corresponding with the beginning Overhand Knots, see Step 1, leaving 5 inch ends.

Note: This belt may also be worked in one solid color, or in any two or three colors, whatever will go with your wardrobe.

What Else You Can Make

The eleven articles for which detailed instructions are given in this book are only a few of the many things you can make for yourself and for your home. Look around. You have mastered the fundamentals of macramé; now design some articles that you want, and which would give you pleasure to make. Here are a few suggestions:

Shopping bag	Hammock
Dog Lead	Cardigan, pullover,
Curtain	jacket
Room Divider	Soap Holder
Earrings	Wall Hangings
Rugs and Mats	Cushion Cover
Braces	Lampshade
Dressing Gown	Shoes
Picture Frame	Guitar Strap
Mobile	Ring or bracelet
Watchband	Ties
Collar	Fringes for hats,
Necklace	ponchos, shawls, etc

Macramé Suppliers

Although the popularity of macramé is rapidly increasing, it is not all that easy to find suppliers who specifically cater for it. This is partly due to the flexible nature of the craft. The basic thread, yarn or cord can, as explained on pages 3 and 4, be almost anything. A little common sense will make it clear, however, that the material should be fairly strong and not too difficult to manipulate, and it will also be obvious that material for a rug or utility bag should be different from a more delicate article like a necklace or a fringe. Advice has been given about home-made knotting boards on page 2. T-pins can be obtained from G. F. Farr & Sons, Ltd. of Luton, but milliner's pins, push pins and glass-headed pins can be obtained from many haberdashery shops and stationers. Beads can be bought from The Bead Shop, 53 South Moulton Street, London W.1., Ellis and Farrier Ltd., 5 Princes Street, London W.1. and Eatons, 16 Manette Street, Soho, London W.1. (who also sell very useful bamboo tubes). Dryads Ltd., of Northgates, Leicester, are used to supplying schools and the general public with various twines (write for particulars and latest prices), and McCulloch & Wallis Ltd., of 25-26 Dering Street, London W.1. are also a most useful contact for piping cord and other haberdashery items (send for excellent catalogue). Suppliers of Rope, String,

Cords to the public include Fletcher, Sons & Co. Ltd., of 439 London Road, Croydon, and G. R. Hurst & Co. Ltd., of Rothschild Street, London S.E. 27. Makers of suitable material include H. G. Twilley Ltd., (Crysette, Lysbet & Goldfingering), and William Peacock Ltd., of Paisley (several excellent Chalk Lines); but these two firms only supply shops for reselling to the public (the former to knitting yarn stores and the latter to hardware shops and builders merchants).

For the ordinary, inexperienced and slightly bewildered beginner no better start could be made than to contact Hobby Horse of 15-17 Langton Street, World's End, Chelsea, London S.W.10. (telephone 01-351-1913). Not merely will they send most helpful catalogues, covering natural and coloured macramé strings; glass, ceramic and specially dyed wooden beads, but they actually have prepared idea sheets for macramé and many other crafts. They are open from Tuesday to Saturday (10.00 a.m. to 6.00 p.m.). Finally, a visit to The Needlewoman of Regent Street, London W.1. is recommended.

NOTE

The Publishers are most grateful to Doris Duckett for checking a number of technical points and in particular for help in compiling the list of suppliers.